Simple Weight

by

Tania Runyan

FUTURECYCLE PRESS
www.futurecycle.org

Second printing.
Only formatting and minor backmatter changes were made.

Published by FutureCycle Press
Lexington, Kentucky, USA

ISBN 978-0-9828612-4-0

For Jeremy

At night I pray: Remain the mute
who silently unfolds in deeds,
who of himself keeps on proceeding,
etching weighty mounts of silences
unto mountains and countenances.

—Rainer Maria Rilke (tr. Annemarie S. Kidder),
"The Book of Monkish Life"

Contents

Blessed Are the Poor in Spirit

I am not made to pray. I close my eyes
and float among the spots behind my lids.
I chew the name God, God, like habitual
gum, think about dusting the shelves, then sleep.

It is hard to speak to the capital LORD
who deals in mountains and seas, not in a woman
rewashing her mildewed laundry while scolding
her toddler through gritted teeth. I should

escape to the closet and kneel to the holy
singularity who blasted my cells from a star.
I should imagine the blood soaking
into the cross's grain, plead forgiveness

for splintering my child's soul. But the words
never find their way out of the dark.
Choirs and candles shine in his bones
while I doze at the door of his body.

Mary at the Nativity

The angel said there would be no end
to his kingdom. So for three hundred days
I carried rivers and cedars and mountains.
Stars spilled in my belly when he turned.

Now I can't stop touching his hands,
the pink pebbles of his knuckles,
the soft wrinkle of flesh
between his forefinger and thumb.
I rub his fingernails as we drift
in and out of sleep. They are small
and smooth, like almond petals.
Forever, I will need nothing but these.

But all night, the visitors crowd
around us. I press his palms to my lips
in silence. They look down in anticipation,
as if they expect him to suddenly
spill coins from his hands
or raise a gold scepter
and turn swine into angels.
Isn't this wonder enough

that yesterday he was inside me,
and now he nuzzles next to my heart?
That he wraps his hand around
my finger and holds on?

Good Friday

The time has come
to write our sins

and nail them to the cross
leaning on the altar.

Silence, except
for a hundred pencils

scratching abuses
and lusts. I write:

*I do not want
to know you.*

Every morning I try to pray
and dream instead

of gardens
I am too impatient to plant:

rose-dripping arbors,
slopes of poppies

taking two years
to flower. It is hard

to seek this dormant
God who buries

his miracles in the soil.
They sleep

until the slow work
of rain and decay

pushes them into
daybreak, when I

am still turning
into the darkness

of my pillow and expecting
nothing to grow.

For Theirs Is the Kingdom of Heaven

Problem was, I had to talk to Jesus
to get there, the man whose giant white robe
flowed through the pages
of my *Golden Children's Bible*.
Oh, the fright of all that sunlit hair,
sheep and children jostling for his arms!
I found my comfort lying alone
on the shaded slope in the yard.
I didn't have to look into the expectant eyes
of Christ, but the magenta clouds of bougainvillea
rolling over the fence. I gathered
the fallen blooms, reading the stories
of drizzle and ants written on the papery bracts.

On a parallel hillside he quieted himself
so he could listen to the universe
in his heartbeat: planets coolly ticking off
their orbits, gills pulsing, electrons darting
in the bread. As the sky began to darken
he sank even deeper into the earth,
his elbows drinking in the green stain of moss.
He exhaled the stricken faces,
the tear-drenched kisses and shouts,
the leprous hands tugging at this sleeve,
and closed his eyes, searching for peace
in the afterlife of shadows.

The Goldfish Pond

I like the dead one best,
my daughter says,

and follows a corpse
the length of her smallest finger
around the edge of the pond.

Among the water lilies
a dozen fish flicker and spark.
Look how pretty, I say.

But she is lost now,
bending so low
her nose almost touches
the scales.

He keeps looking at me.
I love him.

And she reaches into her face.

Sunset of Dust

When the western light saturates our room,
we see that we live in nothing more
than a nebula of dust. We watch the flurries
of our skin shimmer and swirl in the rays,
forty thousand cells a minute sloughing into the cloud.

Once these cells quivered and split
like unkissing lips, then journeyed twenty days
through the epidermis. They rose to their purpose,
as promising as a drift of hellebores cracking the ice.
Now the plumes of our former bodies curl into the air

as we sleep, settling inside our shoes, clinging
to lampshades, succumbing to the acrid rag of Pledge.
Ten percent of our pillows' weight is the bodies
of dust mites sated with our skin, the cobbles
of their droppings stacked between the threads.

Every night we return to their graves
and settle into the darkness. It is about breathing
now, tasting the toothpaste in our kiss,
warming our feet in the down. There is nothing more
to see. We fluff our pillows. We lay down our heads.

Blessed Are Those Who Mourn

Blessed are you, woman,
doubled over in the bathroom stall
awaiting your miscarried child.

Blessed are you, weeping
constellations of all-night vigils
on the shot-up university campus.

Blessed are you, soldier,
rubbing the phantom
of your amputated leg,

and you, small boy, huddled
in the closet with a handprint
on your face—bless you.

Bless the vice in your stomach,
your throat stripped raw from crying,
the shoes you fling across the room.

Bless the rain you curse for falling
so easily outside your window, the chair
you collapse in after a night of pacing the halls.

Bless the food you cannot eat,
the hair you cannot wash,
the God you cannot pray to.

Bless you who want to forget
it ever happened but feel the grave
rising to asphyxiate your heart.

Bless you who want to dive
into the grave and feel nothing
but the simple weight of the earth.

Blessed are you who damn
these words, who send them to hell
with your sorrows.

Blessed, yes, even you.

Markings

When I overstay despair
the desert begins

to whisper in my body.
The smallest grains

scrape along my nerves,
the wind picks up,

and sand twisters whip
through my heart.

It is good to be empty
and alone, the cold night

settling in. My soul tumbles
away on a back road

as I watch the stars rise
clean and sharp

above the mountains.
But always I am left

with a thin cast of dust
on my bones

and God stealing over
to drag his name with his finger.

For They Shall Be Comforted

This oak took its bad news to the heart.
Lightning struck two springs ago
as I snored between my flashing walls.

Now scallops of orange fungus layer
the fissured bark. Spider sacs trailing
ragged webs streak the splinters like comets.

I have lost someone. Her eyes flash
among the decaying leaves. I hear
her small hands fluttering in the creek.

Grieve me, she calls. *Split your heart
with my face.* There is nothing else
I can do. I pull up a broken branch. I sit.

Nursery Theme

Pastel hippos bounce across the wallpaper border.
Ostriches bat their lashes; elephants walk trunk in tail.
Behind them, Noah lifts his staff like a drum major,
and the sequence repeats.

The child sleeps under a bedspread of clouds,
every night on the brink of deluge.
She dreams of her plush animals marching
into a purple boat where they will stomp and sing.

If they insist on arks, they must let her believe
in an endless supply of rainbows and doves.
They must tell her, yes, it's a party from God
where he gathers his friends to sail the world.

She will wake soon enough to birds screeching
in the rafters, lions cringing in the thunder,
the dead beating against the hull.

Anna the Prophetess

Widows of Jerusalem, I too was once
young enough to believe my life mattered.
When I woke, the sun rose for me. I tucked lilies in my hair.
Now I am eighty years a temple dweller.

What a wonder of faith! they proclaim. Truth is,
I cry in the dark. I beg priests for bread

and pick insects from my hem. But today,
an infant came to be blessed. He curled

into the crook of my arm, and when his eyes
wandered to mine, I remembered every hope

stored in my childhood's heart: gazelles
and henna shrubs, doves perched in the crags.

I touched his face—
that skin we were meant to wear forever.

* * *

Widows of Jerusalem, this is what I know.
You are not dying. You are falling slowly

into another world, where bread will grow
from a thousand fragrant fields; where lilies

will clothe you in sunrisen petals;
where everyone will call you beloved child again.

Blessed Are the Meek

She is all we learn to forget,
this woman approaching
the edge of the health club pool.

She wears her hair
like laundry lint. Faded Lycra
toucans and orchids

sag beneath her nipples.
I imagine her going home
to dump a can of Campbell's

in a casserole while her husband
barks orders from the football chair.
She moves through the house

without consequence,
straightening an old lighthouse
cross stitch in the hallway,

rifling through coupons
for half-price oil changes.
But this morning,

she is here. Her eyes take in
the narrow lane of water
as if it were the river

of an ancient civilization
and she plans to wrap her arms
around time itself.

She twists, then stretches
her mottled fingers
to the rising dough of her feet.

She catches my stare,
arches her brows at me
and jumps, gliding

and breathing, gliding
and breathing as I fade
above the churning waves.

Joseph at the Nativity

Of any birth, I thought this
would be a clean one,
like pulling white linen
from a loom.

But when I return to the cave,
Mary throws her cloak
over the bloody straw and cries.
I know she wants me to leave.

There he lies, stomach rising
and falling, a shriveled pod
that does nothing but stare
at the edge of the feeding trough
with dark, unsteady eyes.

Is he God enough
to know that I am poor,
that we had no time
for a midwife, that swine ate
from his bed this morning?

If the angel was right, he knows.
He knows that Mary's swell
embarrassed me, that I was jealous
of her secret skyward smiles,
that now I want to run into these hills
and never come back.

Peace, peace, I've heard in my dreams.
This child will make you right.

But I can only stand here,
not a husband, not a father,
my hands hanging dumbly
at my sides. Do I touch him,
this child who is mine
and not mine? Do I enter
the kingdom of blood and stars?

Girl With Thirteen Necklaces

She clacks and clatters down the stairway,
factory-punched gold medals swinging
from patriotic ribbons, multicolored
plastic squares spilling down her shirt
like Chiclets. A string of pomegranate beads
tangles with a clutch of neon keys. Hundreds
of tiny seeds of glass simmer at her neck.

Is the woman still at the conveyor belt
whose fingers pinched the misshapen lumps
from a harvest of polymer daisies?
Where is the man whose monitor fluttered
with schematics for pink, praying angels?
The inspector who passed the velveteen
ribbon slowly through his fingers: *This'll do?*

The world has made its preparations
to sway above her navel: loggers, barrels,
big rigs, box cutters, mechanical arms
swirling pigment in the paint. She leaps
and spins to the rainstorm of beads.
She flops on the couch and falls asleep
to the beautiful, shifting weight.

For They Shall Inherit the Earth

The child who labored under the AK-47,
who bore its weight like a claw on his naked shoulder

and memorized the equation of trigger + blood = food,
cried out to *Ludana* and escaped to the darkening savannah.

He awoke on a carpet of acacia shadows. Above him,
the coral dawn shook out its feathers

and raptors began to ripple through the sky.
He spilled out like water to the Lord.

And the ants came to him, came by the thousands,
encircling his neck like a chain of glittering onyx.

To Silverfish

I shake out the bath rug,
and you streak the floor like mercury,
whip your tails and ooze
beneath the peeling bathtub caulk.
I can never pinch you in time.

You pinball between shampoo bottles,
unaware that I am the fast one
who slings mascara onto my lashes
while skipping through voice mails
with a baby on my hip.

In the darkness of the cabinet,
you approach one another
with trembling antennae, back away,
approach, and tremble again.
You gently wrap the female

in silk spun from your mouth
and lay a gossamer pillow of sperm.
For three hundred million years
you have done this. Oceans of blue scales
have formed on your bodies

and molted and formed again, the waves
of your spent lives crashing silently
under our feet. You refuse a destination.
I squeal from the driveway as your ancient,
patient bodies smolder in the walls.

My Daughter's Hair

at birth just a few fingerprints
of light on her head

now a red tide washing
down the hallway

a cascade of carrot peels
hot pennies sliding on the dash

where'd she get it they ask
at the playground and store

I shrug   she grabs my leg
and splatters me with her wild paint

but in the sleepy mornings
I take the flaming silks in my hands

still   love   still
let me brush them awhile

let me braid them
before they burn out

Blessed Are Those Who Hunger

On the day that 27,000 children died,
my dishwasher flooded its basin. I cradled a bowl,

running my finger around a yellow shroud of curry.
I mourned the scrubbing I would have to endure,

the salesmen with their litany of buttons,
the snake's nest of disconnected tubes.

Mothers embalmed their children in wet sand.
Fathers folded skeletal bodies in sheets.

The mosquito nets and vaccinations were still
en route, stalled in cargo holds, legislation, hearts.

I did not remember. I opened the dishwasher again
and felt my blood quicken at the sour soup

of food and water, the marinara-flecked plates,
and—Jesus help me—oatmeal stuck to the whisk like bone.

Tiffany Lamp at Nightfall

The stained glass darkens like pooling blood
in a lattice-work of rhombi. The pull chain, still swaying
from my child's last runabout, loses its shadow
to the dusk. Over one hundred years
since the first filament sparked, but still:
Can it be this simple to turn away the night?
Perhaps I am meant to sit in a dark room
and let my sins knock about like these insects
caught in the screen. Perhaps I should search
for those parts of me I've sold to so many glowing things.
But the chain hangs just one elbow-hinge away.
And these drops of brass fall so easily into my hand.

Ultrasound

I peel apart a daylily bud
in its final moments
of darkness. There:

the rolled, yellow petals,
pressing their tips together.
Sticky anthers set

to lay themselves open to bees.
The night before the appointment,
I toss with the branchy shadows.

Finally, this life
will be certain. We see
the blue lungs, the skull, limbs

orbiting wildly around the heart.
It's a girl, the technician says,
and prints her out with a click.

What do I do with this terror
of energy and breath
in my hands? Her picture

throbs in my fingers,
ready to flame into life
or wither into death. I can't

put her down. I want to go
to the lily bed and tuck
the sepals back into place.

For They Shall Be Satisfied

How do I taste and see that the Lord
is good? My rejoicing and my pain
drive me to the frosted freezer doors,
haloed half-gallons shedding

their feathers of ice as I stack
mint chip and sherbet in my cart.
Every day I receive them,
invite them to infuse my blood.

Without the cold, would I still
curl in a chair, afghan on my shoulders?
No spoon in my hand, but a psalm
receiving the spit of my guttural prayers.

And in my midnight despair
just my faltering faith in invisible things,
no dripping carton held to my chest
as I scrape around the edges to the end.

Growing Season

Too much spring rain.
The gutters burst
with hundreds of miniature maples.
They have germinated
in their own rotting pods
and stretch their leaves
to the sun. Yank them out,
I tell my husband,
before the neighbors talk.
He climbs a ladder,
cuts the stems loose
with a trowel.

Outside Beijing, the mother
of our next child
digs all day, hair sweeping
the fine soil where black seeds
roll from her fingers.
More drought, they warn,
but she plants anyway,
for you never know
when a storm will hit.
Today, row markers and dirt.
Tomorrow, plump cabbages
glistening on the table.

Kindergarten Night

Nathan plays violin! a mother bubbles
to me in the hallway.

The kid plunges his fists in his pockets,
scowling through platinum bangs.

You do not know your own perfection,
child. You can still train your fingers

to climb Kreisler's cadenzas
and fold into Bach's double-stops.

My violin leans in the basement.
Twenty-five years ago, the symphony

brought their instruments to class.
I pulled a bow across the open D

and felt something like heat
rising from the earth.

There was no end to my life.
Rosin fell like riches on my shoulders.

Blessed Are the Merciful

Amish schoolhouse shooting, Nickel Mines, PA

I didn't trust their forgiveness.

Before the blood cooled on the schoolhouse floor
they held the killer's widow in their arms,

raised money for his children,
lined his grave site with a row of patient horses.

Somewhere in town there had to be a father
splitting a trunk and imagining the crush

of the murderer's skull. There had to be a mother
hurling a Bible at the wall that received her prayers.

Or is it just the flash and noise of my own life
that primes me for anger? Does scrolling

through playlists in traffic fill the spaces
in my mind reserved for grace?

Forgiveness requires imagination.
Eye for an eye is efficient.

For the man brought chains.
He brought wires, eyehooks and boards.

He brought a bag of candles and lubricant
and secured little girls with plastic ties.

Two sisters begged to be shot first
to spare the others.

He shot them first. Then the rest.
One child with twenty-four bullets.

Perhaps they know something I don't,
something to do with the morning rising

over an open field. The fathers receive
the meadowlark, the swallowtail,

the good corn rising into the fog.
The mothers ride their carriages into town,

accepting the rumbles of the stony road,
tripping into the rough hands of God.

2086: Instructions for My Daughter's Nurse

I know you will be underpaid, your knuckles raw
from scrubbing bedpans. When you walk into the sitting room
heavy with wheelchairs, nothing will seem alive
but the smell of urine. But please, take a moment
to find my daughter among the stone stares.
Go to her, touch her shoulder, and look into her face.
Keep looking when she coughs,
when the phlegm dribbles over her cracked lips.
Smile. Hum softly. For five minutes, adore her.
Within those gray folds of skin are eyes
that once danced around the bright corners
of her nursery, a mouth that parted in wonder
at every leafy shadow on the wall, a face that dazzled
like a newborn galaxy the first time her mother looked down.

Shepherd at the Nativity

Last night I watched another wet lamb
slide into the dark and beheld this same
drowsy beauty: a mother bending toward
her nursing young. New limbs trembling.
Matching rhythms of breath.

The angels told us to praise and adore.
I spend my life trying not to love
such small things. But again and again
I carry my new lambs and name them,
play songs for them on the reed pipe,
bind their broken legs and search for them
in the foothills, until they are sold and worn,
served up, split open on an altar
and I feel my own blood rushing to the edge.

For They Shall Receive Mercy

Heavy with the day's errors
and tired of myself,
I lie beside my napping daughter
and wait for my breath
to drag me closer to sundown.

Stretching in her sleep,
she rests her hand on my back.
I can be hard to release.
But I give myself slowly
to those fingertips—

delicate and water-swept
like an anemone in a tide pool.
The first time I found one
I couldn't stop staring
into its mile-deep eye.

I was twelve, embarrassed
by the crust of pimples
at my hairline. My pants
never quite reached my ankles,
and I sat at the lunch bench alone.

But here: a sun bursting
with green solar flares,
a storm-blown flower—
a creature so beautiful for not
being me. I could dance

on the rocks or crack my head
and drown, and the anemone

would still rest there, calmly
sifting plankton. So I bent
as far as I could and sank

my hand into the cold.
I felt my life bubble up.
The anemone rippled
with an incoming wave—
then our fingers stuck.

Tantrum

We pray fierceness
for our daughters:

slung-shot *no's*
striking down the oppressors,

firestorms raging
in the side-sweeping rain.

My three-year-old
refuses her bed.

I strip her of blankets,
teddy bears, bracelets

and books, all
but her shrieking steel will

that pitches like a thousand
violin strings, her flesh

barely clinging. One
final scream sears the air,

and she reaches, wide-eyed.
She terrifies herself.

I want to take her back,
fold her pink limbs

and tuck her inside me,
where she will sway

and give with my movements
again, her spine bending

like a stalk in the wind
as I walk my steady path.

In Utero

At nine weeks, the book tells me,
the baby is the size of an olive.
Within a month she expands
to a plum, a lime, a peach.
In my dreams brilliant fruits
twist and strain at the stem.

At week fourteen, she becomes
my fist, at seventeen, my hand
spread wide. I close and open
my fingers, watch the shadow
curl in the warmth of my palm.

I wish my body were known
by images, aligned with the world
of things: a six-foot young maple,
a giant neon *I*, a humpback's
glittering fluke. I would glide
in the pulse of dark water,
unaware of destinations,
soothed by the distant winds
above the surface

until I became a self,
without comfort or metaphor,
naked and whole in the burning light.

Blessed Are the Pure in Heart

A new collection of vases shimmers in her window—
hand-blown, smooth as sheets of water, the kind I've always
    loved.
Aqua teardrops, lime flasks, oblong rose and amber bubbles

pour their colors into the hallway and soak her face with light.
In the backyard, two daughters share a tree swing.
In the kitchen, scones-from-scratch steam on crystal tiers.

She opens her arms to receive me. I sink into her cashmere,
and for a moment I love her sincerely, love the perfect fall of hair
on her back, the orchids nodding on mahogany stands.

I want her children to play Carnegie on their way to Harvard
    Med,
her husband to land the corner office. I want vases
to line every table and shelf, turn her home into a brilliant
    cathedral.

Hey God, I think, *I've finally nailed it. Get a load of me!*
Then my eyes fall on the vases again, where the three o'clock sun
boils and spins. My throat constricts. I can never break through
    the glass.

Thirties

We are angry with ourselves.
We have moved into the vinyl houses

springing up in the cornfields.
We scowl in traffic below billboards

for storage boxes. We buy the boxes.
We eat dinner without lifting our eyes,

wash our children, and crawl into bed
with our backs to our spouses.

There might still be years enough
to change the world, we think,

but we want nothing more than sleep,
drifting to the strange new pleasures

we would have never noticed at twenty:
the gratifying click of the thermostat,

branches sweeping the shingles.
In the morning, we look in the mirror

and see the first thin lines spreading
through our faces like the fine roots of oak trees

extending deeper into the earth,
searching for the water hidden there.

For They Shall See God

You kneel in front of a marble headstone
and peer through a baby-shaped porthole.
You see the lake fringed with conifers,
your breath billowing through a fetal frame.

You did not intend to come here.
You do not want to debate or explain.
You just want to stare into the child
you found on your morning walk.

Maple pods spin into her forehead.
Sun shatters in the curl of her feet.
And where the chambers of her heart would be
an egret cries and hurtles to the sky.

Stephen's Stones

He has the face of an angel:
soft, androgynous, fire in his hair.
Roses of blood seep through his mantle
as he reaches an arm out for balance.

The stones continue to weave their flight.
A conglomerate rock, brown flex of muscle,
takes aim at his bowing head.

Once two continents collided,
and a river squeezed through a mountain.
Quartz and calcite fused and spun
a new earth on the bottom of the stream.

The stone has settled in the hands
of a laundress, in the shepherd's fire,
and, briefly, in the sky when a boy
hurled it through a torrent of stars.

Now the stone arcs off Stephen's face.
Blood and sediment cling to his hair.
Quartz glistens, bones crack,
his arm bends under his fall.
Dust to dust to dust.

The Deer

On the country highway
my headlights catch a vision:

a brown paper bag
billowing toward my car—

a Christmas lantern
lifted by the wind?

I swerve—I gasp
in the shine, I brake.

My life is composed
of these split-second

blessings and deaths:
hummingbird flash,

skid of the apple knife—
every moment

flickering at the wick.
I catch myself from slipping

on a sterling plate of ice.
A glowing thing

becomes a fright of bones
colliding with the door.

Blessed Are the Peacemakers

*Clearly, these women would need to have a good deal
of courage. They would need to offer their lives as a
sacrifice. They should be ready to be always at the most
dangerous places and to face as much if not more danger
than the soldiers...*

—Simone Weil,
Plan for an Organization of Front-line Nurses, 1942

A vision: Before I knot the first tourniquet,
a grenade gouges me from earth.
My crushed bones spill out like hourglass sand.

Ms. Weil says the body is meaningless,
that God created me for such a kind death:
perhaps as we die together, a soldier will journey

to his mother, his wife, through my eyes.
I will withhold my name, let him dream in death.
(Why must holy deeds be lonely?)

Offer your anonymity as a gift, she says.
Let the morticians search for tags, shake their heads
about that "young woman from the sky."

Spools of gauze rolled out on the field
will be a testament to the other world.
Forgive me, God, but now I feel nothing

but my heart's dumb thump,
new breasts straining my blouse, naive.
It is too late to run from the plane,
the parachute, the doorway of clouds.
I have seen those pictures from the sky:

small uniforms reaching, shrapnel glowing
like the lanterns at last summer's dances,
when school boys gazed over my shoulder,
dreaming of flight.

Lydia at Dusk

Mosquitoes wove and whined among the moss-
sheeted stones like the violins of ghosts. She
lowered her open insect jar with its yellow,
aged corpses of rolly pollies and cabbage
moths; giant carpenter ants whose mouths
still clutched aphids and leaves; that night's pistils,
bees, earwigs, bark, fireflies that (maybe)
would simmer on her dresser till dawn. The woods
ticked toward darkness. She aimed the plastic
toes of her tweezers at one plump mosquito,
squeezed, giggled at her blood smearing the glass.

After the Storm

Vapors hover over the driveway. My daughter
brushes by the geraniums on the doorstep,
wet petals clinging to her calves. She peels them off

like sunburned skin. Beyond the woods a siren wails,
a red scarf sailing through the fog. *Someone is hurt,*
she says. She sinks her arms into the flooded ditch

until her elbows disappear. I have nowhere
to go. The earthworms have slithered
onto the driveway to save themselves from drowning.

For They Shall Be Called Children of God

I do not concern myself with things
too marvelous for me.

I pull young buckthorn after the rain
and watch the cranesbill fill in,

tie a clover around my child's wrist
to stop her from crying after a fall.

I do not concern myself with matters
too great. I skim the article

once or twice—rebel fighters,
refugees, tankers billowing smoke.

Shall I say each time my eyes wander
to the blue stars of lilacs tumbling

from a jar on the table,
that I love those lilacs more?

I will die being no help to this man
curled around a broken IV

on a floor in Sri Lanka.
I would like to sink into his stare

and pray him through his nightmares.
But first I must lie in the grass

and bury my face in the great skirts
of the sky, making peace

with the carpenter ants and the other
small brilliances of my life.

Sestina for Brood XIII

Five billion nymphs have tunneled from the earth,
slipped out of their ghostly skins
and adorned the trees with their red-laced wings.
A bevy of blenders. Motorboats. Buzz saws,
the articles warned. But from a distance,
their mournful chorus, like a cloud of flutes, rises

beyond the old-growth oaks, rises
to the atmosphere's last hold on the earth.
I drove my daughters some distance
to find them. They collected the skins
from the grass by the pail-full until they saw
the first blood-drop eyes, the first flickering wings.

Gentle, I admonished them. *Their wings
can dissolve in your hands.* They raised
the cicadas to their eyes like prisms, saw
the seventeen-year handiwork of the earth
for one moment resting on their skin.
I told them how the nymphs suckle roots at a distance

of nine feet underground, their bodies distant
particles in the soil. The hope of wings,
the slow, invisible weaving of their skins
lie forgotten as a human generation is raised
in the whir and clamor above the earth:
Blenders. Motorboats. Buzz saws.

When I was thirteen, bored with the universe, I saw
Haley's Comet, a dull, milky smudge in the distance.
My parents reminded me of my rare chances on earth
to see great things: Columbia's mighty wings

on its maiden takeoff, the Olympic flag rising
in our hometown, King Tutankhamun's gilded skin.

I wanted nothing but to inspect my skin
in the mirror. Who cared what else I saw?
Not you, daughters. I know next summer the same sun will rise,
and these cicadas will have flown the distance
of your memory. Their eggs and broken wings
will have completed their lonely burrows into the earth.

But remember, each shed skin is a quarter-distance
of your life. You saw, and a part of you rode away on those
     wings,
rising and falling beyond the reach of the earth.

David Considers His Music

There is nothing too wonderful about it.
I pick it up, I play.
Is that not the life of a harp?

I cannot tell why people change
with these notes. Widows lift their tambourines,
children drop their rocks and stare.
Even the sheep look up from the field
as if they know more than they should.
I think I could turn over a rock
and watch the lichen pulse with each arpeggio.

It is ordinary to be amazing.
I don't try to do anything else.

At times I see the music play before me.
Deep chords become these violet mountains,
heaving from the ground like muscles.
A slow crescendo, the green power of a wave
washing over me, the elation of being small, being lost.

I like to play because I lose my place.
I play yet don't make anything happen.
I lift the harp as easily as grass sprouts around my ankles,
as olive leaves tumble down my back.

I believe I can carry a violet mountain
on my back. This is not amazing.

You see, I can only laugh when children stare
with wonder. I can't help the fingertips
that weave my soul around the strings.

There is something that keeps me awake
at the most beautiful hour, the black sky with light
pressing behind it. I cannot stop leaning over
the verge of possibility.

I think my song will fall through the decades
like a muscle of water. I think it will splash
children, widows and rocks. I think I will weave
my soul around the world. Thank you, Lord,
that I will have nothing to do with it,
that I will do it all.

Blessed Are Those Who Are Persecuted

*—Kund Iverson, drowned by several boys in Chicago
after refusing to steal apples, 1853*

Because God ignited the trees with apples
one August afternoon, enchanting a few boys
who scuffled along the dirt path;
because He made the stream curve by the pasture
where the boys could see Kund
giving his cow a drink in the shade;
because they were created in the image of God,
desiring to surround themselves
with pure and lovely things,
like a shirtful of apples spilling at their feet;
because like God they had ideas
and muscles strong enough to pile hay to the sun
and hold a child under water;
because the stream rose that spring
after a curtain of silken rain;
because Kund would just not stretch his hands
into those branches, gripping a law
as real as stone under his fingertips;
because when they let him up to change his mind,
his lungs suddenly awash with air,
he shook his head and held Moses'
glittering tablets to his chest, sinking
below the lily pads and cattails;
because on this summer day
an enormity of beauty collided
with a few mistakes; because of this, a woman
is covering a damp body with kisses,
begging her son to wake for dinner.

Dear Spectator

—Telemachus, Martyr to the Gladiators

Again, you bring your family and stare
into the dirt, deaf to the earth's gentle language.

Did you know when the first man fell,
the child in your arms tugged your sleeve,
a green beetle flickered around your toes?

Listen. Real exhilaration comes slowly
and quietly, like deep breaths
of rainy air in the evening.

This young man trembling in his armor
will surprise no one when his neck snaps
under the lion's paw. You expect his blood
to trace rivers around his body.

But imagine the wonder of his possible
life: praying on a hillside
through the changing shades of sunrise,
touching the face of his newborn son.

Listen. God knows when the sparrow falls.
You too will take notice again.

I will enter the ring in my hermit's robe,
step between the warriors and take the blade.
My sacrifice will shock you,
but it will make you look away
at last, hear the wind rustling the branches,
cheer when the shadows sweep
over the Colosseum walls.

For Theirs Is the Kingdom of Heaven

When my friend tells me of the man
who nailed his dog's paws to the kitchen floor
after she urinated there
I don't know what makes me more angry:
the story or that my friend chose to share it.

Because now the picture won't dissolve:
the curious brown eyes, tail swishing
as the man returns from the garage
with the hammer and nails.
The man calm enough to think,
yes, I will hold this leg steady
as I pound through the yelps.
And as one paw shatters and blood
seeps into the cracked tiles,
I will not stop but proceed to the next.

Perhaps I should not resist
replaying the scene in my mind.
If the dog had to suffer torture,
shouldn't I at least remember it?
The man hammers away.
The dog does not understand betrayal.
Worse, she vanishes in the privacy of pain
as the world spins on without her.
No one can slip inside the flesh
she was born trusting
and feel the instant of nail piercing skin,
bones shredding muscle and nerve.

It is over now; all suffering
eventually ends. Unless I keep it alive.
Unless I visit that lonely kitchen
and search for the rusty nails.

Ursula's Virgins

—St. Ursula and 11,000 virgin companions,
martyred by the Huns in Cologne.

A sudden gust punches the sails.
Our ship meanders and tips,
then pulses steadily
toward the Cologne shore
like blood returning to a heart.

I don't cry out
when the waves burst over
the railings. We look down
in silence, sinking our fingers
in each other's arms.

The storm enters us.
I try to keep my dress down,
pressing the fabric to my thighs.
Ursula looks to the sky,
mouth open. Her face breaks
into a patch of roses.

The green shore grows.
Men's voices rumble over the hill,
then the rain of a thousand swords.
I should be folding my hands
in prayer, but all I can do
is tuck the loose hair
behind my ears, let my hand linger
at the nape of my neck.

Angel at the Nativity

Oh, God, I am heavy
with glory. My head thunders
from singing in the hills.

This night will come once.
Enough bright lights.
Enough shouting
at shepherds in the fields.

Let me slip into the stable
and crouch among
the rooting swine.
Let me close my eyes
and feel the child's breath,
this wind that blows
through the mountains and stars,
lifting my weary wings.

Grasshopper

You plunge your arms
in the voltage of insects

and remove your hands
in prayer. Between

your knuckles the angles
and flecks of a Kiowa

grasshopper flicker
in the ruddy dark.

Then stillness. Indigo
stars of spiderwort

kindle in the prairie
smoke. The hind

legs tighten. We feel
the tendons extending,

the slick springs
snapping into place.

Gravity. Fire.
In your hand:

a singularity.
You open your palms

and we leap
to the infinite edge.

Blessed Are You When Others Revile You

We knew Preacher Man had it all wrong,
the 6'4" senior who pinned kids to their lockers
with the Four Spiritual Laws,

popped his head into classrooms
to proclaim "all have fallen short
of the glory of God," and waved his Bible

as teachers dragged him to the principal's
office, pages riffling like the hems
of Jesus in the desert.

We knew he had lost the point
of sharing the Gospel through the simple
testimony of a life well-lived:

turning down sex and weed,
spotting spare dollars in the lunch room.
He makes us look so lame,

we groaned in youth group.
He's working against our cause.
But when one afternoon

a freshman stuck his foot out
and Preacher Man slammed to the floor,
only to scramble after the retreating boy

and pull him into a hug, I knew
I had it all wrong, because he became
Jesus in the hallway of my school,

and I could never forgive him.

Invasive

Don't learn about the plants you see;
their splendor's just a vibrant lie.
Everything lovely is a weed.

I picked the sprawling chicory,
its petals sliced from the summer sky.
I hadn't learned about this plant. You see,

that wild parsnip makes you bleed
when it brushes by your sunburned thigh.
Now all that lovely gold is weed,

and buckthorn, too, with emerald greed
chugging the woodland's soil dry.
Don't learn about the plants you see,

like purple loosestrife spouting seeds,
blazing, rampaging six feet high.
Everything lovely is a weed.

I used to have no guides to read,
just roamed and gazed with simple sighs.
Don't learn about the plants you see,
for everything lovely is a weed.

Esau's Explanation

Since sunrise, I had speared wild goats in the fields.
So when I smelled Jacob stirring the red lentil stew,
my body tore open with hunger.

This is the smell I absorbed in my clothing as a boy:
lentils bursting in the boiling pot,
the spiced fragrance of the earth after summer rain.

Every morning, mother rinsed and sorted the lentils,
turning them in the water like bright river stones.
I always grabbed a few and flung them in the air,

watched them scatter the dirt in fiery constellations.
Later, as we scooped hot stew to our mouths
I laughed at the lentils still clinging to her hair.

And during those nights of screeching windstorms,
I didn't even have to run to her. I slept in my cloak,
breathing the smell of the earth, her hair, the river, the rain.

Why tell my story of impulse and greed?
I sold my birthright for stew. No matter. This food is more
than a word or a promise. It keeps me alive

in the open spaces, knits together the marrow of my bones.
So my stomach was empty. God too saw a void
and couldn't help himself. He had to fill it—scatter it with stars.

For Their Reward Is Great in Heaven

If at the end of it all we receive new bodies,
if we hold our breath without consequence
and pass our hands through one another

without any pain, what will be our reward?
Elephants plod hundreds of miles
to the Okavango Delta to feel the floodwaters

surge into their tributaries of skin. The factory worker
turns thousands of bolts to feel her husband
peel off her socks and knead the hours from her feet.

I need to suffer, God. I need to go my own way
so that you can search for me under the brush.
Will you sometimes hide your face from me in heaven,

sew up the temple curtain so I can kneel crying
at the hem, fabric in my fists? Will you let me
dream of those old hungers that brought me dizzy

and desperate to a trough of muddy pods, the sins
that made you run to me with a robe and fattened calf
while I stumbled and bled, still a long way off?

Acknowledgments

I wish to express my grateful acknowledgment to the following publications in which these poems (some in earlier versions) first appeared.

Arts & Letters: "My Daughter's Hair," "Kindergarten Night"
Atlanta Review: "2086: Instructions for My Daughter's Nurse"
Autumn Sky Poetry: "Blessed Are Those Who Hunger"
The Christian Century: "Blessed Are the Poor in Spirit," "For They Shall Be Comforted," "For They Shall Inherit the Earth"
Confrontation: "Sestina for Brood XIII"
Indiana Review: "The Goldfish Pond"
Innisfree: "Blessed Are the Meek," "Blessed Are Those Who Mourn," "Blessed Are the Merciful"
The Monongahela Review: "Girl With Thirteen Necklaces," "Grasshopper"
Natural Bridge: "Esau's Explanation"
New Orleans Review: "Growing Season"
Poetry: "Blessed Are the Peacemakers" (as "The Night Before")
Poetry Northwest: "David Considers His Music"
West Branch: "Tiffany Lamp at Nightfall"
White Whale: "In Utero"
Willow Springs: "Mary at the Nativity"

The following poems also appear in the chapbook *Delicious Air,* published by Finishing Line Press: "Mary at the Nativity," "Nursery Theme," "2086: Instructions for My Daughter's Nurse," "Blessed Are the Peacemakers" (as "The Night Before"), "David Considers His Music," "Blessed Are the Persecuted" (as "The Martyrdom of Kund Iverson"), "Dear Spectator," "For Theirs is the Kingdom of Heaven" (as "Memorial"), "Ursula's Virgins," and "Esau's Explanation."

Cover art by Ivan Ivanov; author photo by Roxanne Marie; cover design and typography by Diane Kistner; Legacy Sans text and titling

About FutureCycle Press

FutureCycle Press is dedicated to publishing lasting English-language poetry books, chapbooks, and anthologies in both print-on-demand and Kindle ebook formats. Founded in 2007 by long-time independent editor/publishers and partners Diane Kistner and Robert S. King, the press incorporated as a nonprofit in 2012. A number of our editors are distinguished poets and writers in their own right, and we have been actively involved in the small press movement going back to the early seventies.

The FutureCycle Poetry Book Prize and honorarium is awarded annually for the best full-length volume of poetry we publish in a calendar year. Introduced in 2013, our Good Works projects are anthologies devoted to issues of universal significance, with all proceeds donated to a related worthy cause. Our Selected Poems series highlights contemporary poets with a substantial body of work to their credit; with this series we strive to resurrect work that has had limited distribution and is now out of print.

We are dedicated to giving all of the authors we publish the care their work deserves, making our catalog of titles the most diverse and distinguished it can be, and paying forward any earnings to fund more great books.

We've learned a few things about independent publishing over the years. We've also evolved a unique, resilient publishing model that allows us to focus mainly on vetting and preserving for posterity poetry collections of exceptional quality without becoming overwhelmed with bookkeeping and mailing, fundraising activities, or taxing editorial and production "bubbles." To find out more about what we are doing, come see us at www.futurecycle.org.